EAGLES OF NORTH AMERICA

CANDACE SAVAGE

EAGLES
of North America

GREYSTONE BOOKS

DOUGLAS & McINTYRE PUBLISHING GROUP

VANCOUVER/TORONTO/NEW YORK

00 01 02 03 04   5 4 3 2 1

Second edition 2000

This book was originally published by Western Prairie Producer Books, a book publishing venture owned by Saskatchewan Wheat Pool. First Douglas & McIntyre printing 1992.

Greystone Books
A division of Douglas & McIntyre Ltd.
2323 Quebec Street, Suite 201
Vancouver, British Columbia
Canada V5T 4S7

Canadian Cataloguing in Publication Data

Savage, Candace. 1949 –
    Eagles of North America
    Includes bibliographical references and index.
    ISBN 1–55054–783–6
1. Bald eagle. 2. Golden eagle. I. Title.
QL696.F32S29 2000   598.9′42   C99–911243–0

Cover design by Peter Cocking
Text design by John Luckhurst/GDL
Front cover photograph by Kevin Schafer/Tony Stone Images
Back cover photograph by Corbis
Printed and bound in Canada by Friesens
Printed on acid-free paper ∞

The publisher gratefully acknowledges the support of the Canada Council for the Arts and of the British Columbia Ministry of Tourism, Small Business and Culture. The publisher also acknowledges the financial support of the Government of Canada through the Book Publishing Industry Development Program (BPDIP) for its publishing activities.

To Diana

Acknowledgments

This book owes its beginnings to Rob Sanders; its orderly creation to Jane McHughen; and its beauty to the photographers who have contributed their work.

The information and insights reported in the text are the creation of several generations of naturalists and biologists, including those whose names are noted in the reference list. Although much remains to be learned about eagles, the existing body of knowledge is an impressive accomplishment that bears testimony to the discipline, patience, intelligence, enthusiasm — and physical courage! — of these researchers.

With this book, we owe a particular debt to two of these eagle-enthusiasts and experts, Dr. Jon Gerrard of Headingly, Manitoba, and Dr. Stuart Houston, of Saskatoon, Saskatchewan, who shared their reference materials and reviewed the text for errors. Any remaining inaccuracies or omissions are, of course, the sole responsibility of the author.

In addition, personal thanks are due to Diana Savage for her patience and help and to Richard Clarke for listening.

Foreword

In most parts of North America an eagle is a bird to be pointed out to anyone within calling distance. It is one of the few birds to attract the notice of the average citizen who would deny any interest in, or knowledge of, birds. Yet the inveterate bird lister is almost as happy to tick off the thousandth eagle as the first. The excitement does not pall. No one can ignore an eagle.

I thrill to the sight of an eagle on its home territory, whether a majestic Bald at a northern lake or a magnificent Golden along river breaks. Both offer a challenge to me. For the past twenty-five years I have sought them out on their home ranges in order to band their young. In my years of working with eagles, I have banded nearly two hundred nestlings in order to learn how far they travel and how long they live.

The obstacles a bird bander must overcome are many. Picture a Bald Eagle nest 5 feet high, built at the very top of an 80-foot tree with few or no branches. Imagine the excitement of climbing up, roping oneself securely to the trunk below the nest, and reaching to the extent of one's long arm to grasp the leg of an eaglet and apply a band. Equally frightening and initially just as hazardous is the hand-over-hand descent of a rope to a Golden Eagle nest perched partway down a sheer 150-foot clay cliff. Experiences such as these have given me a particularly vivid appreciation for the work of the photographers in this book, who have skillfully captured images of eagles in their natural surroundings.

The thrill generated by eagles is enhanced by their environment. The Bald Eagle is associated with pristine northern lakes and rugged coastlines, some of the last places in the world where the air is unsullied and the water pure. In such haunts the visitor leaves worldly cares behind; tension, insomnia, and poor appetites are unknown.

The Golden Eagle nests in picturesque river valleys; mountain forests; and isolated lands of cliffs and rolling hills, cactus and sage. It is possible to spend a whole day in such surroundings without meeting another soul. Wherever it may be, Golden Eagle country is a fine retreat from the madding world.

The essence of this feeling for eagles and their environment has been captured by Candace Savage. Her three-pronged technique involves a careful search of the literature, a rigorous selection of beautiful photographs, and the preparation of an eminently readable text — a winning combination. I am sure that anyone who shares my feelings of awe and wonder for these magnificent birds will welcome this sensitive treatment of the eagles' world.

C. Stuart Houston

Eagles circle
to the sun,
spread wide wings
and rise,
tracing spires
of sky

Earthbound,
we fade
to tiny specks
beneath
their spiral
flight.

Introduction

In our everyday world of human-made, human-scale things, we are inclined to think rather well of ourselves. We are *homo sapiens,* after all, and even in this day of evolutionary enlightenment generally view ourselves as favored offspring of the universe. It takes an eagle to bring us down to size. Though only a fraction of our weight, these birds dwarf us; for by soaring into the sky, they give a tangible, vertical dimension to the observable world. They offer us a measure of the heavens and, as they disappear above the clouds, hint at spheres beyond our sphere to which we have no ready access. Perhaps we are not the center of things after all, not so very large, not so powerful. With all the finesse of modern technology, we can't ride the air like the eagles. We can't even come close.

It won't surprise you to learn that eagles have long had an exalted place in the religious and political symbolism of humankind — for if these birds impress us, think how they looked to our ancestors, when flying machines were a fantastic dream. Judging from the historical record, the natural human response to eagle flight is awe. Very early in our cultural development, these feelings began to give rise to a constellation of inspiring, if unscientific, associations and beliefs. Eagles inhabited the highest regions of the air;

they lived on the sacred ground of the mountain tops. Surely they were favorites of the gods and companions to the life-giving sun. They alone, it was said, could gaze unharmed at the sun's brilliance; and they were reported to expose their offspring to its heat, so that any weaklings might die. Was it an eagle who first brought fire to Earth; and did the fiery phoenix give its eagle-kin a claim to immortality?

Eagles were intermediaries between heaven and earth, the link between human and divine. In particular, they became associated with the regal sun god and, in Roman times, were attributes of Zeus, the capricious king of Olympus. Themselves impervious to lightning, they alone were able to grasp their master's wrathful bolts. When Zeus took a fancy to Ganymede, it was an eagle who fetched the young man from Earth. For that service, the birds were immortalized in the northern sky as *Aquila,* the eagle stars. When the gods wanted to send a portent of military victory or future greatness, they often chose eagles as their messengers. Accordingly, eagles have a long history as a symbol of earthly power. In Babylon, Egypt, and Persia; Greece, Rome, and Constantinople; even (according to Marco Polo) in far-off Georgia, eagles were a mark of kingship and, sometimes, of personal divinity. More than two thousand years ago, the eagle was selected as the ensign of the Roman legions, an emblem of divine favor to lead them into war. Centuries later, when Alexander the Great was born, two eagles soared over his palace to show that he was a son of Zeus who would someday rule a double kingdom in Europe and Asia. During the Middle Ages, in the heyday of falconry, eagles were reserved by royal decree for the use of emperors and kings. From Gilgamos of Babylon, through Genghis Khan, Charlemagne, and Napoleon, eagles have represented divine favor and divine right. Even in our own century, the Austrian Empire entered the First World War under the eagle's wing. Today, of course, an eagle appears on the seal of the United States, though with different connotations, as an emblem of sovereignty.

Eagles also have a central place in the spiritual traditions of native North Americans. From one end of the continent to the other, we find eagle emblems, eagle totems, eagle clans; eagle-feathered headdresses, arrows, medicine bundles; eagles in myth, in song, in dance. Everywhere the birds are celebrated as creatures of vision, power, and grace. Clearly, eagles have an impact on the human imagination that crosses cultures and time. In fact, the impulse to view these birds as larger-than-life continues to affect the way we think and feel even today. For some people, it contributes to an attitude of reverence and respect, so that killing an eagle becomes a sacrilege. Others are led in the opposite direction to view the birds as supernaturally cruel killers, which pillage the lower orders of life and deserve to be wiped out. But if eagles have a message for people today, and many would argue they do, we will not find it in heroic half-truths at either end of the scale. As people of a scientific age, we must begin with the facts.

First, a few basic definitions. An eagle is a powerful diurnal raptor. A raptor? A bird of prey. Diurnal? Active during the day. An eagle, then, is a powerful bird of prey that is active by day. There are nocturnal raptors, too, better known as owls, but they belong to an entirely different group and won't concern us here. The eagles' nearest relatives are the hawks, kites, buzzards, vultures, and falcons with which they share the Order Falconiformes, a grouping of about 275 species world-wide. Of these, something like 60 are called eagles, though they are not a unified group. Eagles are called eagles because — "they just sort of look like eagles." They range in size from the formidable Harpy Eagle of South America, which weighs up to twenty pounds (eight kilograms) and spans seven and a half feet (two meters), to the well-named Little Eagle of New Guinea, which is smaller than a gull. From a taxonomic point of view, the term "eagle" has little significance.

The Falconiformes are the avian equivalent of carnivores, specialized to hunt and eat meat. Accordingly, they are well-armed. Their principle means of offense are their large, dagger-clawed feet, with which they grasp and pierce prey. The wicked-looking hooked beak is used for tearing carcasses apart. (People who handle eagles always go for the feet first, grabbing the birds by the lower legs to ensure that the talons are under control.) To make the most of this weaponry, the birds also have special adaptations to help them find prey. Their eyesight, for example, is thought to be exceptional, perhaps five or six times more acute than our own. Imagine being able to see a rabbit crouched in a meadow more than a mile (two or three kilometers) below. Eagle-eyed, indeed! They also have better depth perception than many species of birds because their eyes are oriented more towards the front than the sides of the head. As a result, their left and right fields of vision overlap through an arc of about thirty-five to fifty degrees in front of the face. (A pigeon, by contrast, has only twenty-four degrees of overlap.) What is the advantage of this enlarged span of two-eyed, or binocular, sight? To find out, try looking out the window with both eyes open, then with one eye closed. What happens to your ability to judge distances? Think what a difference this could make to an eagle striking prey.

In addition to weapons and acute senses, a good hunter also must be able to travel long distances with ease. Flapping flight is a lot of work. That's no problem for seed-eaters, whose food is concentrated, plentiful, and occurs in clumps. But for a meat-eater, whose meals are hard to catch and miles apart, it takes too much energy. Many species of raptors, including most eagles, have solved this problem by becoming specialists at soaring. As anyone who flies small aircraft can tell you, the air has contours which, though more plastic than those of the land, are predictable. For soaring birds, the most significant features in the "airscape" are areas of upward-moving air that provide lift. These occur in two ways. First, winds are deflected upward when they run into a barrier — a cliff, a line of hills, a wall of trees along the edge of a river or lake — creating a lane of lift on which broad-winged birds can ride. The location of these "freeways" is relatively stable, given the lay of the land and the direction of the prevailing winds. The Hawk Mountain flyway in Pennsylvania, where thousands of migrating raptors are seen each year, is a perfect example of this phenomenon. The second source of lift draws its energy from the sun. Uneven heating of the air just above the ground causes the formation of "thermals," spiraling columns that rise to considerable heights (and are often topped by cumulus clouds). For eagles and other soaring birds, thermals serve as escalators. Once the birds have attained sufficient height, they swoop out and down, relying on the momentum of their descent to propel them to the next column of upwelling air. If the thermals happen to be drifting themselves, pushed along by the wind, eagles can travel twenty miles (thirty kilometers) an hour — effortlessly. And this is only a measure of their ground speed: since most of the distance they cover is vertical, they are actually traveling faster yet. Wide wings and a broad tail, to catch the air, and slotted wingtips, which can be adjusted for stability, are the basic equipment of these masters of soaring flight.

Two species of eagles are known to breed in North America: the Golden Eagle, *Aquila chrysaetos* (which is simply a fancy way of saying "golden eagle"), and the Bald Eagle, *Haliaeetus leucocephalus* ("white-headed sea-eagle"). At weights of around thirteen pounds for a female and ten for a male (five and four kilograms, respectively), and wingspans of up to seven and a half feet (more than two meters, slightly less for a male), they are the largest of the broad-winged raptors that occur on this continent. Though both are adapted for soaring, the Golden is credited with special excellence in flight. With a flick of the tail, a tilt of the wings, a sensitive adjustment of the wingtips, it can maneuver through skittish air currents along a hillside or sail steadily into a fierce wind. Except for nestlings, the species can be recognized by the regal mantle of feathers on the crown and nape, which give it its name (and, no doubt, many of its mythological associations as well). If you can get close enough, which isn't likely in the wild, you can also tell a Golden by its feet, which are feathered right down to the toes. Bald Eagles, like other sea eagles, have bare legs. When soaring, the Golden can usually be identified by a quick estimate of body proportions: if the head is less than half the length of the tail, it is likely a Golden, not a Bald, Eagle.

Golden Eagles are birds of the high country. Probably the most numerous eagle of their size in the world, they are at home at a variety of exotic addresses across Eurasia, North Africa, the

Middle East, southwestern China, India, Pakistan, Korea, and Japan, as well as in North America. Wherever they occur, they are typically associated with mountains and rugged terrain, where the relief of the land promotes the development of updrafts and thermals. On this continent, the species once bred widely but is now extinct in many areas. During the nesting season it is common only in the west and northwest, with a particularly vigorous summertime population in the southern Yukon. In the winter, the pattern changes somewhat, as birds from the north shift to more moderate latitudes. Birds that nest in mid-continent remain on or near their breeding grounds year-round. As a result of this doubling-up, relatively dense wintertime populations develop in the American mid-west and New Mexico — with up to twenty thousand birds in Wyoming alone — mostly around grasslands and open valleys where prey is abundant. Smaller numbers are found at this season in the eastern United States, particularly along the coastal plain, between Maine and Chesapeake Bay, and on the Appalachian plateau. Here they rely on steep river valleys, marshlands, and waterfowl sanctuaries to supply their winter food.

Golden Eagles prefer to eat rabbits and hares. They can, and do, catch many other small and medium-sized creatures, such as marmots, ground squirrels, moles, mice, muskrats, skunks, weasels, badgers, herons, hawks, coots, ducks, magpies, meadowlarks, hawks, snakes, fish — the list goes on and on. They are even capable of taking quite large prey, including pronghorns, coyotes, lambs, calves, and fawns; but rarely do. Their basic meat-and-potatoes fare has long, floppy ears and a short-cropped tail, with grouse and carrion running a close second. Accordingly, their hunting range includes open brushland and scrubby meadows where these animals can be caught. And caught. And caught. On average, a breeding pair requires about seven hundred pounds (over

three hundred kilograms), live weight, of food each year.

Breeding eagles don't wander at random in their search for food, but confine themselves within a familiar hunting ground, or "home range." In California, for example, a pair of Goldens may hunt over thirty or thirty-five square miles (eighty or ninety square kilometers); while in a dense northern forest, where meadows are small and far apart, they often require six or seven times that area. Their basic hunting strategy is cat-like surprise. Alert to every movement within range of their telescopic sight, they ride the updrafts in silence, ready to swoop onto their prey at split-second notice. Or they may fly close to the ground, using features of the land to keep them from notice until the last moment. One eagle was in the habit of taking coots in this way, sailing into the area by a devious route and then descending to ground level where she could use a fence as a blind. Another paced alongside a moving truck to gain advantage on unsuspecting waterfowl. Sometimes eagles hunt in pairs, one near the ground, flushing prey from cover, and the other at a height, ready to pounce. Overall, they are only successful about one time in five, but it's obviously enough to get by on.

In summary, a Golden Eagle can best be pictured soaring over rugged countryside, with a rabbit clutched in its talons. A Bald Eagle, on the other hand, should be imagined on a commanding perch along the shore of an ocean, river, or lake, searching for fish. Compared to a Golden, an adult Bald Eagle has a larger head and shorter tail, features which may be related to its slightly less graceful flight. If the head is more than half the length of the tail, the bird is likely a Bald, not a Golden. This rule is probably least useful in identifying youngsters, which have different body proportions from the adults. First-year birds have extra-long tails (and wings) and are easily confused with Goldens. Even experts make mistakes.

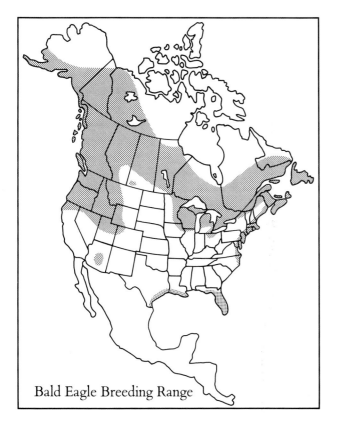

Bald Eagle Breeding Range

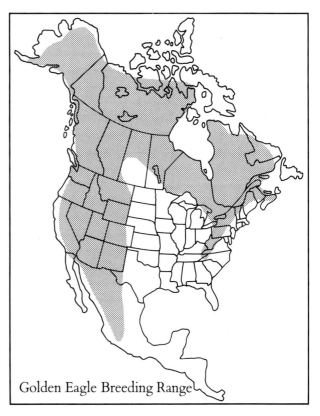

Golden Eagle Breeding Range

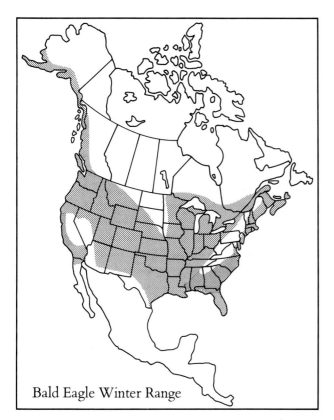

Bald Eagle Winter Range

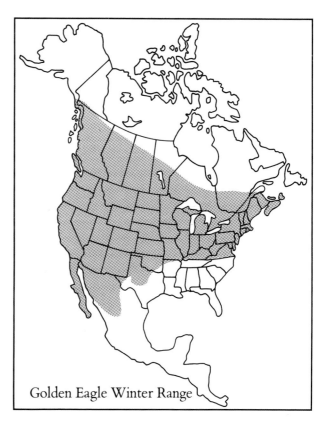

Golden Eagle Winter Range

The difficulties are multiplied by the fact that juveniles (Bald Eagles up to four or five years of age) go through a succession of white-and-brown plumage stages in which they scarcely resemble the adults. These youngsters can be recognized in flight by patches of white at the "wingpits." Fortunately, the adult birds are unmistakable, with their brilliant white heads and tails, and Roger Tory Peterson is quite right to describe them as "all field mark." An exclusively North American species, the Bald Eagle is most abundant in Alaska and British Columbia, where two-thirds of the population occurs, but significant breeding populations also inhabit the forested areas of other western provinces and states. Other important breeding areas include Florida, Chesapeake Bay, the north Atlantic coast from Maine to Newfoundland, and the Great Lakes states. It may be worth mentioning that Bald Eagles which nest in northern regions are noticeably larger than those which breed in the southern United States.

Like Goldens, Bald Eagles are only partially migratory. Those that have access to open water will stay on their nesting grounds year-round, but if the countryside freezes over, the eagles fly south or to the nearest coast. Once again, most winter sightings are in the west, with concentrations in British Columbia and the Pacific states and along the Mississippi and Missouri rivers and their tributaries. One odd-ball exception is found in Florida, where Bald Eagles nest in November and December. Some of these birds then migrate as far north as the Atlantic provinces in the summer months! The timing of migration is generally assumed to be regulated by hormones, which in turn are thought to be influenced by changes in temperature or day-length. So how do these Florida eagles get things "backwards"? No one can say.

Bald Eagles will eat almost any animal that they can get, be it mammal, bird, or fish, and have even been known to raid bread and pastries from a garbage dump. Their preference, however, is for fish, with waterfowl as an important secondary food. In their own way, they are spear-fishermen, watching for their quarry from a perch or an aerial height, then swooping down and grabbing it. Usually, there is little drama associated with this process — swoop, snatch, and away we go — though sometimes the birds plunge into the water when they make the strike. If they become waterlogged or their prey is too heavy to lift, they simply swim to shore, using an overhand movement of the wings that is rather like the butterfly stroke. They can catch seabirds by dropping down over the waves and using the swells as cover to catch their prey in flight. Diving ducks are often forced to submerge again and again until they are too tired to resist capture.

Much of the Bald Eagle's food requires less skill to obtain. The birds have no objection to carrion, and at certain places and times are about as predatory as Turkey Vultures. Their other main source of food is theft, both from other meat-eating species and other Bald Eagles. These facts dismayed Benjamin Franklin, who expected eagles to set a higher standard of behavior. The Bald Eagle, he said, was a bird of bad moral character and should not have become America's national bird; he recommended the honorable turkey instead.

Moral judgments aside, piracy and other social interactions among Bald Eagles continue to spark interest among eagle-watchers today. A species like the Golden Eagle, whose prey tends to be dispersed (rabbits don't generally occur in herds!), can be expected to be relatively solitary, as is indeed the case. But for the Bald Eagle, which often exploits prey that occurs in "clumps" — more than enough to feed one individual — there is sometimes an advantage to sociability. This is particularly true in the wintertime when ice and snow impose their grim austerity. Bald Eagles sometimes meet this challenge by gathering where food is abundant, at fish runs, for example, or waterfowl sanctuaries (birds injured by hunters make easy prey). In the Chilkat Valley of Alaska, more than three thousand Bald Eagles congregate each fall to feed on the spent bodies of spawning chum salmon. Even where their feeding is more dispersed, wintering birds often get together to rest at night, taking shelter in a stand of conifers. Some of their traditional wintertime roosts accommodate up to four hundred eagles per night, and birds will fly long distances just to join the group. These gatherings appear to facilitate "information sharing," since inexperienced or underfed individuals can follow their more successful companions to good feeding grounds. Are social purposes fulfilled here as well? Do mates follow, and hence assist, each other? Do young birds follow their parents? Are new pairs being formed? So far, no one can answer these intriguing questions.

If sociability makes it easier for eagles to locate food, it also has a cost — increased competition for every mouthful that is found. "Fast food" is a way of life for wintering Bald Eagles: grab it and go, eat it on the wing. Otherwise someone will take your meal away. Where food is plentiful, it's common for an eagle to drop what it's eating or walk across unclaimed fish in order to steal from another bird. These takeover attempts are usually successful; and this is not by chance. The birds observe one another closely and "assess" the likelihood of victory. Is the competitor large or small, flying or perched? Does its crop (the sac in the neck where food is held for grinding) look full or empty? Is the other bird extending its head and wings in an aggressive display? Is it calling? If the opponent has the edge in size, height, hunger, and aggressive intentions, the outcome is assured, and both birds know it. The food transfer takes place without a fight. Although this scrapping may look foolish when food is ample, it presum-

ably makes more sense during a famine. Then, survival depends on grabbing whatever you can, and "well-mannered" birds will die. This powerful selection pressure probably explains why the behavior is so well established in Bald Eagles.

Ritualized conflict of this sort is common throughout the living world and may be especially important for predators such as eagles, which could do each other great harm. During the breeding season (roughly March to October in mid-latitudes), both Bald and Golden Eagles seek privacy for rearing their young. In the spring, each pair takes up residence in an area that offers suitable places to nest and roost and the promise of sufficient food to rear a family. Although hunting grounds on the margins of this zone may be used by neighboring pairs, other eagles are not regularly found in the vicinity of the nest, especially when there are young. This even spacing is achieved with very little outright hostility. Often simple possession of the area is enough: Bald Eagles, for example, choose exposed perches, where their glistening white heads can be seen from far and wide. Other eagles may simply choose to avoid the area, knowing that it is occupied. The same message is transmitted through territorial display, which in both species takes the form of an undulating aerial ballet of zestful ascents and daredevil stoops, performed by a single bird or both members of the pair. This is a conspicuous way of announcing that an area has been claimed and would-be settlers will have to look elsewhere. Some researchers think that these performances are sexually specific, amongst Golden Eagles at least, with males displaying against intruding males and females repelling females. Spectacular free-fall descents, in which two Bald Eagles lock talons and cartwheel toward Earth, also occur. Though sometimes interpreted as courtship, many careful observers believe these are ritualized encounters between residents and trespassers. This behavior is quite rare, since most intruders leave as soon as they're confronted by a resident bird.

The undulating flight display may also play a role in courtship, the social and physiological process by which a pair prepares to breed. Most of the time, however, the mated pair simply live quietly together on their home range, perching, preening, hunting, and nest building. When the female is ready for copulation, she makes a head-down, bowing gesture, and the male hops on her back, with his talons closed so that she won't be hurt. As he flaps his wings for balance, her tail goes up, his down, and their cloacas touch. Eagles sometimes copulate "out of season," too, when it couldn't have anything to do with fertilizing eggs. Maybe this is one of the ways in which the special loyalty between mates is maintained, as it is for ourselves. In any case, pair bonds between eagles are thought to be long-lasting. Both Bald and Golden Eagles tend to breed with the same partners and in the same areas in successive years.

Nests may also be used year after year and, since the birds add to them annually, sometimes become enormous with time. One exceptional Bald Eagle nest eventually measured over eight feet across by twelve feet high (about ninety square meters) and probably weighed about two tons. Both species build primarily with sticks, which are carefully woven into place with the bill; the interior bowl is lined with fine twigs and other soft materials. Bald Eagles usually build in large, open-crowned trees near water, though they may choose cliffs or even, exceptionally, nest on the ground. Goldens generally prefer cliffsides, though they readily take to trees, usually beside clearings where they can hunt. Often their nests are strewn with (or constructed of!) rabbit bones. Early in the season, before laying begins, a pair of either species may investigate or refurbish several nests before choosing one to use that year. A pair of Golden Eagles may have as many as twelve nests on its breeding territory.

Eagles are quite variable in this aspect of their breeding behavior: they may or may not have alternate nests, and they may or may not use them in alternate years. Some pairs don't even nest each year.

Interruptions in nesting are probably more common amongst Golden than Bald Eagles. This is because Goldens have to contend with erratic variations in the availability of their preferred food. In many parts of North America, the numbers of rabbits and hares follow a rollercoaster course of valleys and peaks, from die-off through recovery to die-off again. One might expect the population of adult Golden Eagles to be equally unstable, but this does not seem to be the case. Rather than continue to breed as usual when prey is scarce, many Golden Eagles respond to a low rabbit year by failing to nest. With fewer mouths to feed, more of the mature birds will survive to breed another year, and the population is maintained on a more-or-less steady footing.

Both Bald and Golden Eagles lay a clutch of one to three eggs, usually two. Often the second egg appears two or three days after the first, but incubation begins with the first one laid — facts that become vitally significant as the weeks pass. Among Goldens, most of the incubating is done by the female, whose larger body size may suit her to the task. The male takes on a greater or lesser share of this obligation, depending on his inclination to offer and the female's to accept. His primary responsibility, however, is hunting, and here his lesser weight and relatively large wings may give him an edge of ease and agility. Nobody understands why female raptors are bigger than males, but this is one plausible explanation. (A more equal division of labor appears to be usual among Bald Eagles.)

The dozy routine of incubation lasts for five or six weeks. Then, one day, one of the eggs starts to chirp, and the incubating parent stands up to peer at it. Over the following hours or days, the youngsters struggle out of their shells, emerging in the same order as they were laid, to sprawl prone at their parent's feet, a bedraggled mass of feet and bills. Even from a distance, an observer can tell that hatching has occurred, because the adults, who to this point have flattened themselves snugly onto the nest, now habitually adopt a more erect stance that makes room for the nestlings. Too weak to stand, too poorly insulated to keep themselves warm, the youngsters command almost constant attention for the first couple of weeks. Golden Eagles maintain the same basic division of labor as before, with the male bringing in prey and the female offering it to the young in bite-sized bits. A little later, when the young have their first crop of feathers, the female will hunt as well. Among Bald Eagles, nest duties continue to be more equally shared. Stepping gingerly around the nest on clenched feet, adults of both species offer the nestlings shelter from storms, cool night air, and intense daytime heat.

Curiously, eagles generally fail to protect their young against another significant peril: one another. Because the nestlings hatch in sequence, eaglet number one gets a head start on development; and with a growth-rate of up to a pound (five hundred grams) every four to five days, this amounts to a marked advantage. If conflict develops amongst the nestlings, as it often does, the winner cannot be in doubt. For certain raptors, the Crowned Eagle and Verreaux's Eagle of Africa, for example, this set-up invariably results in the death of the younger eaglet. The adults go to all the trouble of laying two eggs and hatching two young, then stand passively by and watch the big one peck, bully, and starve the little one to death. Amongst Bald and Golden Eagles, the situation is more complex, since fratricide is a variable occurrence. Both species are capable of raising two, sometimes three, young; and Bald Eagles often do. But for Golden Eagles,

fratricide appears to be the general rule. Fifty to 80 percent of second-born Golden Eagle chicks disappear, mostly within the first two weeks of life.

How are we to understand this behavior, which seems perverse and even cruel from a human point of view? Biologists point out that these deaths must be understood as an aspect of the population ecology of eagles. Over tens of thousands of years, brood-size has been regulated through natural selection to ensure the maintenance of the population. Species that rear one young do so because that is what works best. When a second egg is laid, it is likely insurance against the possibility that the first will fail to hatch. For species like Bald and Golden Eagles, which raise a variable number of young, fratricide is thought to provide a mechanism for adjusting the yearly "production" in accordance with the food supply. Some biologists speculate that this mechanism may also be sensitive to the wintertime experience of the adult birds. If a female overwinters badly, is she more likely to lay a larger, female embryo first? Does she wait a day longer before laying her second egg? Either event could set the stage for immediate fratricide, in a year when the adults are not strong enough to feed a large brood.

Whatever the explanation, the blunt fact is that these deaths are not particularly regrettable. Most eagles die young. By the time they leave the nest, at about ten weeks of age, they look and act formidable, having attained adult size and more-than-adult energy; even their parents seem to find them a little intimidating! But they are far from ready to survive on their own and continue to rely on the adults for feedings. A skilled hunter is made, not born; and young eagles struggle under a heavy burden of inexperience. Though able to fly, thanks to hours of play and practice on the nest, their huge wings still seem unwieldy. Uncertain of the air, they miss perches, crash into branches, or land with such force that they flip upside down. During their first summer, fledgling Bald Eagles spend a lot of time perched like chickens on the ground. Though their skills improve with time, their general lack of know-how can be fatal, particularly during the winter and other food shortages. Perhaps 50 percent of Bald Eagle fledglings will survive their first year, and the survival rate of young Goldens may be lower still.

Obviously, this slow rate of reproduction is sufficient to sustain the population, under natural conditions. Eagles that survive the difficulties of adolescence may live for many years: both Bald and Golden Eagles have been known to approach age fifty in captivity. Even in the wild, many pairs are able to breed for at least eight or ten years, long enough to replace themselves with two mature offspring. Under natural conditions. But what happens if the birds become marked for extinction by human beings with guns? What happens if their food supply is accidentally contaminated with pesticides that interfere with their ability to breed? What if human use of the countryside expands without consideration for the eagles' needs? Does their low rate of productivity put them in special jeopardy? Unhappily, we can answer these questions from experience.

In living memory, Golden and Bald Eagles have decreased significantly in numbers and range. In the eastern parts of the continent, where both species have been hardest hit, Bald Eagle populations have dropped by half to two-thirds in the last twenty-five years. With a total population of about seventy thousand birds, the Bald Eagle is listed as endangered in forty-three states and threatened in five others. The Golden Eagle, with a continental total of about sixty thousand, has been eliminated from the mountainous regions of the eastern United States and is designated as threatened or endangered in Ontario, New York, South Carolina, Tennessee, Alabama,

and North Dakota. While there are convincing signs of a resurgence for both species and even indications that eagles are beginning to reoccupy parts of their former breeding ranges, the birds are believed to be well below their historic populations.

The cause of this decline has been human activity. Except for areas that have proven intractable for development, the surface of North America has undergone a massive rearrangement in the past two hundred years. In the process, eagle habitat has been lost to cities, farms, dams and reservoirs, roads, railroads, aircraft flight paths, lumbering, power lines, mines, oil and gas installations, recreational developments, and other human purposes. In addition, eagles have been victims of direct persecution. During the first half of our century, both species were subjected to a continent-wide shoot-off, in which untold thousands were killed. In Alaska, where bounties were offered from 1917 to 1952, more than a hundred thousand eagles were shot. In the southwestern states, the twenty-year death toll, from 1942 to 1962, was at least twenty thousand Golden Eagles alone, probably more. One man boasted of having killed twelve thousand eagles himself. And it was all thought to be in a good cause. "Everybody knew" that eagles were rapacious predators and that Golden Eagles in particular went around murdering poor innocent lambs and calves, taking food out of human mouths and money out of ranchers' pockets. The only good eagle was a dead one, and so they were killed. But the facts as we now have them point to different conclusions. Quite apart from our new appreciation of the role of predators in natural systems, we can see that Bald Eagles were innocent bystanders in this war, while Golden Eagles were and continue to be of great benefit to ranchers. By preying on rabbits and other small herbivores, they remove animals that compete with livestock for food. Most of their suspected livestock kills are actually taken as carrion. Unfortunately, this understanding came a little late, after both species had been greatly reduced in number and range. Although the birds are now protected by law — it is illegal to kill either Golden or Bald Eagles — gunshot continues to be a principal cause of death. In addition, significant numbers are accidentally trapped and poisoned by baits set for other animals. Electrocution on power lines and lead poisoning, from eating waterfowl that have been shot or that have picked up lead pellets for their crops, are also problems.

One difficulty that Golden Eagles appear to have been spared, at least on this continent, is pesticide poisoning. This is not because they enjoy any special immunity (in Scotland, Golden Eagles were severely affected when their diet became contaminated with dieldrin, used in sheep dips) but because their food supply has not been seriously tainted. Bald Eagles, as we all know, have been less fortunate. As early as the 1950s, Charles L. Broley, an amateur eagle-watcher and retired banker from southern Manitoba, then resident in Florida, was sounding the alarm: "I am firmly convinced," he wrote, "that about 80 per cent of the Florida bald eagles are sterile." Where he had banded 150 young in 1946, he could locate only one in 1958 "and I drove 100 miles down the coast before I found it." Broley thought he knew what was wrong: "For the past decade, Florida has been heavily sprayed with insecticides," and fish dying in Tampa Bay had been determined to contain "a large residue of DDT. An eagle is naturally going to catch the most sluggish fish and is it not possible that a cumulative amount of DDT in eagles has caused sterility?" In this, of course, he turned out to be substantially correct, though more than a decade passed before DDT was banned in Canada, in 1970, and the United States, in 1972. Today, biologists are cautiously concluding that the danger has past. But they are becoming increasingly concerned about the potential effects of acid rain, particularly on birds in eastern Canada and the northeastern United States. As lakes acidify, heavy metals such as mercury and lead concentrate in fish. If acid rain is not controlled, will the Bald Eagles be poisoned again? Will we act quickly enough to prevent irreversible harm?

Judging from past experience, we have reason for hope. Both Bald and Golden Eagles have proven to be remarkably adaptable and resilient. When the slaughter stopped, they were able to increase. When no longer subjected to harmful chemicals, they began to breed again. Under these improved conditions, it has even been possible to increase Bald Eagle numbers in several states — New York, Pennsylvania, New Jersey, and Tennessee, among others — by importing young birds from areas with more vigorous populations, such as Alaska, Saskatchewan, and Manitoba. Taken from their home nests as infants, the birds are airlifted to their new location, reared in captivity with minimal human contact, and released when ready to fly. Despite all the disruption of handling, banding, airplane rides, and confinement in apartment-style nest boxes, the birds suffer no more than natural mortality. Many learn to hunt on their own, find mates, establish territories and rear young, just as if they were natural residents.

Obviously eagles are capable of tolerating a reasonable amount of intrusion and change. In general, they are quite willing to share their habitat with us, provided that we make appropriate allowance for their needs. One way this has been accomplished in recent decades is through the protection of crucial nesting and wintering areas, such as the Snake River Birds of Prey Natural Area in Idaho and the Jackson Canyon Eagle Roost Site in Wyoming. But compromise, and creative solutions, are often possible on a smaller scale as well. An American coal company, about to destroy a cliffside nest site, demonstrated that the eagles could be induced to breed on an artificial platform instead. A power-transmission line in Idaho has designed its towers to provide Golden Eagle nest sites, and the birds have happily moved in. Bald Eagles have been known to share their woods with lumbermen and to continue breeding at a favored site if a 200-yard (meter) buffer is left undisturbed. Cabin-owners and vacationers may be able to occupy eagle habitat, such as shorelines, without causing disturbance, if their numbers are restricted and important habitat such as nest trees, roosts, and feeding grounds are preserved. Screens of vegetation around buildings also help to maintain the eagles' privacy. Obviously, successful coexistence calls for sensitive land-use planning, a willingness to study the habits of individual birds — and common sense. If something we're doing causes chronic disturbance, we must stop doing it. We have to keep our distance, and avoid flushing the birds unnecessarily, particularly when the nestlings are young. Although eagles' ability to tolerate intrusion varies from individual to individual, they seldom demand solitary possession of their world, if only we will take an intelligent interest in their well-being.

In the long run, of course, the eagles' welfare is closely akin to our own. If eagles have a message for us, it is this: we are not alone on this continent. We are not alone on Earth. If we choose to build over or plow up the natural variety of our planet, it is not only eagles who will lose by our action. We will lose as well. If we expel poisons into the environment, it is not only eagles who will suffer, for we will eventually poison ourselves. No matter how high the smokestack or how deep the pit, we cannot export our wastes into some other realm. They will seep up into the water — our water; they will rain down through the air — our air. The environment does not merely surround us: it is us. It enters us through all our senses; we drink it in at every pore. If other living things are being harmed, we are as well. Eagles remind us of our vital connections, and our fragility; and so, as they have through the ages, they bring us close to the sources of life and the powers beyond ourselves that are our sustenance.

The special excellence ...

Mastering the sky: With
outstretched wings a sub-adult
Bald Eagle comes in to land and
an adult Bald Eagle swoops away,
a fish clutched in its talons *(right)*.

... of eagles ...

Powerful strokes of the wings and
daring plunges earthward are all
part of the eagles' repertoire.

... is flight.

Two species of eagles are known to breed in North America, the Bald Eagle and the Golden Eagle. In addition, two of the Bald Eagle's Eurasian cousins occasionally visit our coasts, the Steller's Sea Eagle *(left)* and the White-headed Sea Eagle.

Meet the Bald Eagle. In all the world, Bald Eagles are found only in North America.

Left: **The heroic reputation** of the Bald Eagle can distract us from the truth about its habits and way of life. Eagles are no less wonderful for being what they are.

Feather care is a year-round preoccupation for eagles, as for other birds. This Bald Eagle restores its grooming.

Left: **Shorelines and fish** are two of the usual features of the Bald Eagles' world.

Golden Eagles, by contrast, are birds of high country and broken habitat. This is true wherever they are found throughout the Northern Hemisphere.

Overleaf: **An impression of power:** a Golden Eagle half-spreads its wings to protect its kill.

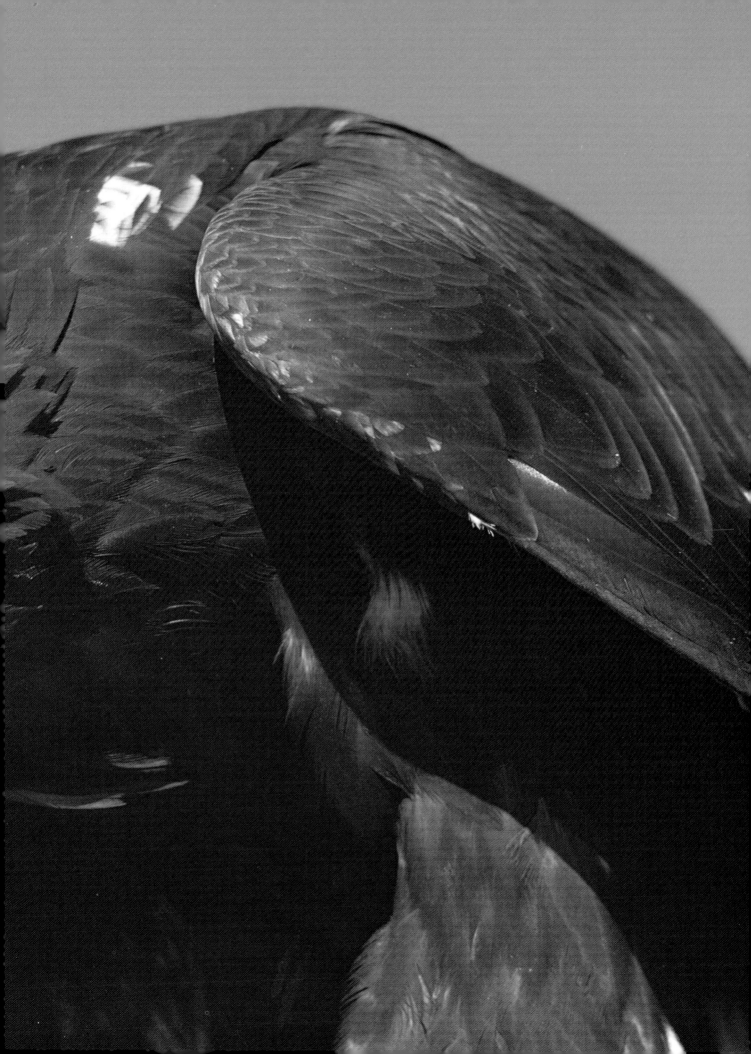

Left: **An intimate view** of a Golden Eagle preening. The burnished cape on the head and neck give the species its name.

Scouring the countryside, this Golden Eagle hunts for rabbits and other small mammals.

Left: **An eagle's talons** are its weapons. As large as a man's hand, they are strong and dagger-sharp.

The surprise of an aerial attack is the Golden Eagle's usual strategy for making a kill.

The hooked bill is used to pull prey apart. This eagle has killed a ground squirrel.

Right: **A Golden "mantles"** and screams in defense of its meal. Of the two North American species, Goldens are generally less vocal.

Overleaf: **Jackrabbits** are the principal prey of Golden Eagles throughout much of their range.

Left: **The fur flies** as the eagle begins its meal.

Other mammals, such as marmots, are included in the Golden Eagle's diet.

Large animals, like deer, are usually taken as carrion. Although Golden Eagles have been known to kill large mammals, they very seldom do so.

Right: **A healthy Golden Eagle** requires about two hundred pounds (ninety kilograms), live weight, of food each year.

Less solitary than Golden Eagles, Bald Eagles sometimes congregate where food is plentiful. These birds are hunting for mice.

Birds, especially waterfowl, are an important secondary food for Bald Eagles. This scrawny youngster may be showing the effects of inexperience as a hunter.

Scavenging is a way of life for the
Bald Eagle. Carrion and garbage
are entirely acceptable foods.

Perch and pounce is the Bald
Eagle's hunting strategy, whether
the perch is on a branch or in the
air.

Left: **Still fishing** is another typical behavior of Bald Eagles. Bald Eagles can even swim, using an overhand movement of the wings reminiscent of the butterfly stroke.

Effortlessly, this Bald Eagle snatches a fish in one talon. Golden and Bald Eagles are capable of carrying the equivalent of their own weight in flight.

The massive beak, as noted earlier, permits the eagles to rip their prey into bite-sized bits. Tearing prey is hard work and Bald Eagles prefer to eat animals that have already been torn open. The bird on this page is readily identifiable as a juvenile by its plumage.

Especially associated with the Pacific coast, Bald Eagles also inhabit lakeshores and forests across the continent. Everywhere, their staple food is fish. The bird on the left is enjoying a crappie.

Overleaf: **Bald Eagles congregate** for winter, sometimes by the thousands. Nowhere are they more numerous than in the Chilkat Valley of Alaska.

Under the stress of winter
conditions, Bald Eagles take
advantage of the few remaining
areas with open water. Life is hard
for eagles at this time of year, and
human disturbance can have
serious consequences.

Sociability is an important theme of
the Bald Eagle's life in the winter.
Calls and displays are common on
the communal feeding grounds.

The brilliant white heads of adult Bald Eagles help the birds keep an eye on one another. In the winter, they take special note of other eagles' success at locating food.

Overleaf: ***Keen-eyed and intent,*** a Bald Eagle perches over a meal of frozen salmon.

When food is plentiful, Bald Eagles may consume almost two pounds (nine hundred grams) at a single feeding.

The relationship between immature birds, like the one on the left, and adults is particularly interesting in the wintertime. Some researchers think that the immatures, motivated by the ever-pressing hunger of youth, are likely to win contests over fish, while others believe that the adults are dominant.

Overleaf: **Squabbles over food** are usually won by the attacker, who takes account of a variety of behavioral cues in assessing the likelihood of success.

A tumultuous feeding scene, like the one on the left, can quickly be transformed into a scuffle. Eagles very rarely injure one another in these conflicts, because the contest is settled quickly.

Displays, like the behavior shown here, are an indication that the bird is emphatically interested in protecting its meal. The more a bird displays the less likely it is to be attacked.

Aerial attacks on eagles carrying fish are not uncommon. Bald Eagles frequently steal food from other species of meat-eating birds as well. Here, an adult eagle attacks a juvenile.

Left: **Golden Eagles** usually maintain their solitary lifestyle in the wintertime. Birds from northern latitudes and high elevations generally shift to more moderate climates for the season, while others remain in their home area year-round.

Nesting activity often begins before the snow is gone. This Golden Eagle has collected a twig for its nest.

Left: **Eagles mate for life,** some researchers claim. But the fact is that no one knows for sure how long pairs remain intact. Whether or not mates stay together throughout the winter is also unclear. It seems safe to say that mate relationships are relatively long-lasting and that at least some pairs stay in touch year-round.

A late snow has not discouraged this pair of Bald Eagles from its vigil at the nest.

81

With dexterity and skill, Bald
Eagles gather twigs and weave
them into their nests. After several
years' occupancy, eagle nests
become enormous.

Sweeping homeward, a Bald Eagle carries grasses to line its nest.

Right: **At home in the heights,** eagles take readily to dizzying nest sites. Either species may nest on cliffs, though it is more common for Golden Eagles to do so.

Tree nest sites may be chosen by
either species, as these
photographs testify. Bald Eagle
nests, like the one on the right,
may be the largest structures built
by a single pair of birds.

Parental duties include both the patient service of incubation and the more vigorous occupation of nest defense. To the right, an immature eagle is seen repelling a raven. People risk life and limb when they photograph eagles, and every image captured on film defies the odds. Aerial behavior is especially difficult to catch. Around nests, of course, such scenes would typically involve adult birds.

Nestlings hatch in the order they were laid, so an age difference of two or three days is not unusual. This may contribute to fatal conflict between siblings, especially in Golden Eagle families. The Golden Eagle chick in this nest is three days old.

Young eaglets are tended by their
parents with great gentleness.

A Golden Eagle chick has little to
do but eat and grow *(left)*. This
bird is three and a half weeks old.
Three weeks later, the same
youngster shows off the emerging
plumage of its all-but–
unmanageable wings.

Left: ***Approaching flight,*** this Golden Eagle nestling wears its first plumage. Over the next several years, it will go through a succession of mottled coats before attaining mature plumage in its fourth or fifth year.

At home on the tundra, a young Bald Eagle surveys its spacious home. In the absence of more conventional nest sites, Bald Eagles settle on the ground.

Overleaf: ***Well-provisioned*** and nestled on a comfortable mat of moss, a young Bald Eagle pants in the hot spring sun.

Large broods like this comical trio
are relatively common among
Bald Eagles.

Panting helps young Bald Eagles to keep cool. Nests built high in trees have the advantage of good visibility, but the trade-off is that the young are exposed to the heat of the sun.

Overleaf: ***As young eagles grow up,*** they become more intimidating, even to their parents.

Hunters are made, not born. Under the watchful eye of an adult, a young Bald Eagle discovers the difficulties of landing.

A separate species? No, the awkward and bedraggled young birds in these photographs are, of course, juvenile Bald Eagles.

Intelligence and experience are the prerequisites for survival by eagles. The Bald Eagle on this page is in its first fall, while the dashing young creature on the right is probably about three years old.

Overleaf: ***Young Golden Eagles***
sometimes remain near the nest
from which they fledged for up to
two years. The patch of white
marks this individual as a
sub-adult.

Mastering their wings, young Bald
Eagles prepare to share in the
grace and strength of their kind.

Death often comes to eagles through human means, whether unintentional or deliberate. In this near-fatal accident, a Golden Eagle has become entangled in the entrails of a road-killed deer. Many eagles are still killed purposely, like this individual swinging from a trap that was especially set to take it. Although the bird on the right has died in maturity, the mortality rate is highest in the first few years of life.

To the ancients, killing an eagle was a sacrilege. Here, a three-year-old Bald Eagle *(left)* and a mature Golden display the alertness and beauty for which eagles have long been revered.

Magnificent, a Golden and a Bald
Eagle display their full adult
plumage.

The mystery of eagles ...

Our knowledge of eagles is constantly expanding. Ultimately, though, there are limits to what we can hope to know.

... is within us and around us.

Patrolling the mist, an adult Bald
Eagle wings its way down a
valley.

The mystery of eagles
is the mystery of life.

References

The breeding range map for the Bald Eagle is based on the map in *The Wonder of Canadian Birds* by Candace Savage; that of the Golden Eagle is derived from the map in K. D. de Smet, "A status report on the Golden Eagle (*Aquila chrysaetos*) in Canada," Committee on the Status of Endangered Wildlife in Canada, 1986. The winter range maps for both species are based on maps in *Field Guide to Birds of North America*, National Geographic Society, 1987.

Adam, C. I. G. 1982. Cliff nesting Bald Eagles in northern Saskatchewan. *Blue Jay* 40: 105-8.

Andrew, J. M., and Mosher, J. A. 1982. Bald eagle nest site selection and nesting habitat in Maryland. *J. Wildl. Manage.* 46: 383-90.

Bell, R. E. 1982. *Dictionary of classical mythology.* Santa Barbara: ABC-Clio.

Bird, D. M., ed. 1983. *Biology and management of Bald Eagles and Ospreys.* Ste. Anne de Bellevue, Que.: Harpell Press.

Boekker, E. L., and Ray, T. D. 1971. Golden Eagle population studies in the southwest. *Condor* 73: 663-67.

Bortolotti, G. R. 1984. Physical development of nestling Bald Eagles with emphasis on the timing of growth events. *Wilson Bull.* 96: 524-42.

———. 1986. Evolution of growth rates in eagles: sibling competition vs. energy considerations. *Ecology* 67: 182-94.

Broley, C. L. 1958. The plight of the Bald Eagle. *Audubon* 60: 162-63, 171.

Brown, L. 1970. *Eagles.* London: Arthur Barker.

Brown, L., and Amadon, D. 1968. *Eagles, hawks and falcons of the world.* 2 vol. New York: McGraw-Hill.

Brown, L. H., and Watson, A. 1964. The Golden Eagle in relation to its food supply. *Ibis* 106: 87-100.

Carnie, S. K. 1954. Food habits of nesting Golden Eagles in the coast ranges of California. *Condor* 56: 3-12.

Clark, W. S. 1983. The field identification of North American eagles. *Amer. Birds* 37: 822-26.

Collopy, M. W. 1983. Foraging behavior and success of Golden Eagles. *Auk* 100: 747-49.

———. 1984. Parental care and feeding ecology of Golden Eagle nestlings. *Auk* 101: 753-60.

———. 1986. Food consumption and growth energetics of nestling Golden Eagles. *Wilson Bull.* 98: 445-58.

Craighead, J. 1976. Sharing the lives of Golden Eagles. *National Geographic* 132: 420-39.

Dekker, D. 1983. The Bald Eagle — hunter or scavenger? *Alta. Nat.* 13: 43-45.

———. 1985. Hunting behavior of Golden Eagles, *Aquila chrysaetos,* migrating in southwestern Alberta. *Cdn. Field-Nat.* 99: 383-85.

Deonna, W. 1955. Deux études de symbolisme religieux. *Collection Latomus* 18.

de Smet, K. D. 1986. A status report on the Golden Eagle (*Aquila chrysaetos*) in Canada. Committee on the Status of Endangered Wildlife in Canada.

Dixon, J. 1909. A life history of the northern Bald Eagle. *Condor* 11: 187-93.

Dixon, J. B. 1937. The Golden Eagle in San Diego County, California. *Condor* 39: 49-56.

Edwards, T. C., and Collopy, M. W. 1983. Obligate and facultative brood reduction in eagles: an examination of factors that influence fratricide. *Auk* 100: 630-35.

Ellis, D. H., and Power, L. 1982. Mating behavior in the Golden Eagle in non-fertilization contexts. *Raptor Res.* 16: 134-35.

Finley, W. L. 1906. The Golden Eagle. *Condor* 8: 4-11.

Fischer, D. L. 1985. Piracy behavior of wintering Bald Eagles. *Condor* 87: 246-51.

Franklyn, J., and Tanner, J. 1970. *An encyclopedic dictionary of heraldry.* Oxford: Pergamon Press.

Fraser, J. D.; Frenzel, L. D.; and Mathisen, J. E. 1985. The impact of human activities on breeding bald eagles in north-central Minnesota. *J. Wildl. Manage.* 49: 585-92.

Gerrard, J. M. 1973. The Bald Eagles in Canada's northern forests. *Nature Canada* 2(3): 10-14.

Gerrard, J. M., and Gerrard, P. N. 1982. Spring migration of Bald Eagles near Saskatoon. *Blue Jay* 40: 97-104.

Gerrard, J. M., and Ingram, T. N. 1985. *The Bald Eagle in Canada: proceedings of Bald Eagle Days, 1983.* Apple River, Ill.: Eagle Foundation.

Grier, J. W. 1969. Bald eagle behavior and productivity responses to climbing nests. *J. Wildl. Manage.* 33: 961-68.

Grubb, T. C. 1971. Bald Eagles stealing fish from Common Mergansers. *Auk* 88: 928-29.

Hancock, D. 1964. Bald Eagles wintering in the southern Gulf Islands, B.C. *Wilson Bull.* 76: 111-20.

Hansen, A. J. 1986. Fighting behavior in Bald Eagles: a test of game theory. *Ecology* 67: 787-97.

Harmata, A. R. 1982. What is the function of undulating flight display in Golden Eagles? *Raptor Res.* 16: 103-110.

Houston, C. S. 1985. Golden Eagles nesting successfully in trees. *Blue Jay* 43: 131-33.

Keister, G. P., and Anthony, R. G. 1983. Characteristics of Bald Eagle communal roosts in the Klamath Basin, Oregon and California. *J. Wildl. Manage.* 47: 1072-79.

Keister, G. P.; Anthony, R. G.; and Holbo, H. R. 1985. A model of energy consumption in Bald Eagles: an evaluation of night communal roosting. *Wilson Bull.* 97: 148-60.

Knight, S. K., and Knight, R. L. 1983. Aspects of food finding by wintering Bald Eagles. *Auk* 100: 477-84.

McMahan, J. 1968. Ecology of the Golden Eagle. *Auk* 85: 1-12.

Merrell, T. R. 1970. A swimming Bald Eagle. *Wilson Bull.* 82: 220.

Meyburg, B. 1974. Sibling aggression and mortality among nestling eagles. *Ibis* 116: 224-28.

Millsap, B. A. 1986. Status of wintering Bald Eagles in the conterminous forty-eight states. *Wildl. Soc. Bull.* 14: 433-40.

Millsap, B. A., and Vana, S. L. 1984. Distribution of wintering Golden Eagles in the eastern United States. *Wilson Bull.* 96: 692-701.

Nelson, M.W. 1982. Human impacts on Golden Eagles: a positive outlook for the 1980s and 1990s. *Raptor Res.* 16: 97-102.

Olendorff, R. R. 1975. *Golden eagle country.* New York: Knopf.

————. 1976. The food habits of North American Golden Eagles. *Amer. Midl. Nat.* 95: 231-36.

Orians, G. H. 1980. Why are Bald Eagles bald? Proceedings of the Washington Bald Eagle Symposium, June 14-15, 1980, pp. 3-14.

Peterson, R. T. 1961. *A field guide to western birds.* Boston: Houghton Mifflin.

Postovit, H. R.; Grier, J. W.; Lockhart, J. M.; and Tate, J. 1982. Directed relocation of a Golden Eagle nest site. *J. Wildl. Manage.* 46: 1045-48.

Servheen, C. 1976. Bald Eagles soaring into opaque cloud. *Auk* 93: 387.

Sherrod, S. K.; White, C. M.; and Williamson, F. S. L. 1976. Biology of the Bald Eagle on Amchitka Island, Alaska. *Living Bird* 15: 143-82.

Stalmaster, M. V., and Gessaman, J. A. 1984. Ecological energetics and foraging behavior of overwintering Bald Eagles. *Ecol. Monographs* 54: 407-28.

Swenson, J. E.; Alt, K. L.; and Eng, R. L. 1986. Ecology of Bald Eagles in the greater Yellowstone ecosystem. *Wildl. Monographs* 95: 1-46.

Terres, J. K. 1980. *The Audubon Society encyclopedia of North American birds.* New York: Knopf.

Thompson, S. P.; Johnstone, R. S.; and Littlefield, C. D. 1982. Nesting history of Golden Eagles in Malheur-Harney Lakes Basin, south-eastern Oregon. *Raptor Res.* 16: 116-122.

Tjernberg, J. 1985. Spacing of Golden Eagle *Aquila chrysaetos* nests in relation to nest site and food availability. *Ibis* 127: 250-55.

Tripp, E. 1970. *Crowell's Handbook of Classical Mythology.* New York: Crowell.

von Volborth, C. A. 1973. *Heraldry of the world.* New York: Macmillan.

Watson, A., and Rothery, P. 1986. Regularity in spacing of Golden Eagle *Aquila chrysaetos* nests used within years in northeast Scotland. *Ibis* 128: 406-8.

Wilson, F. P. 1970. *The Oxford dictionary of English proverbs.* Oxford: Oxford University Press.

Photography Credits

Index